## To:

...............................................

## From:

...............................................

IT'S A GIRL!

Published in 2012 by Struik Inspirational Gifts
New Holland Publishing (South Africa) (Pty) Ltd
(New Holland Publishing is a member of Avusa Ltd)
First Floor, Wembley Square
Solan Street, Gardens
Cape Town 8001

Reg. No. 1971/009721/07

Project management and selection by Reinata Thirion
DTP by Sarah Butler
Cover design by Sarah Butler
Images on pages 7, 13, 18, 22, 25, 27, 33, 36, 39, 58, 62, 73, 82,
91, 93, 105 by LEB Photography; www.lebphotography.co.za;
http://www.facebook.com/lebphotography
All other images from Shutterstock
Printed and bound in China

ISBN 978-1-4153-2114-0

www.struikinspirationalgifts.co.za

# it'sa girl!

A baby is
like the beginning
of all things . . .
**wonder,**
**hope** and a
**dream**
of possibilities.

**– Eda J le Shan**

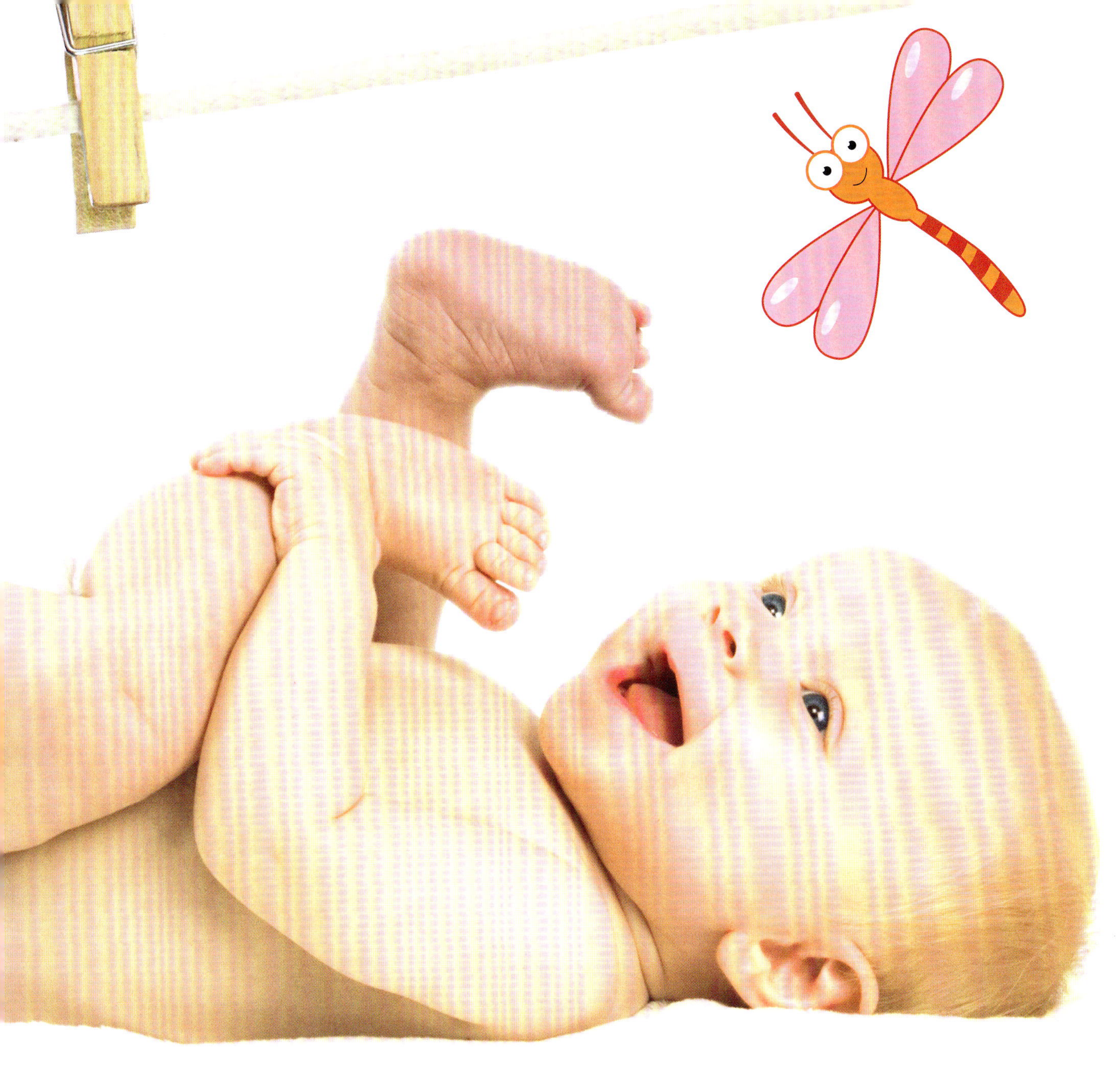

Little girls dance their way

## into your heart,

Whirling on the tips of angel wings,

Scattering gold dust and **kisses** in our paths.

— Author Unknown

If one feels the need of something grand,

*something infinite,* something that makes

## one feel aware of God,

one need not go far to find it.

I think that I see something deeper, *more infinite,*

more eternal than the ocean in the expression of the

## eyes of a little baby

when it wakes in the morning and coos or laughs

because it sees the sun shining on its cradle.

*— Vincent Van Gogh*

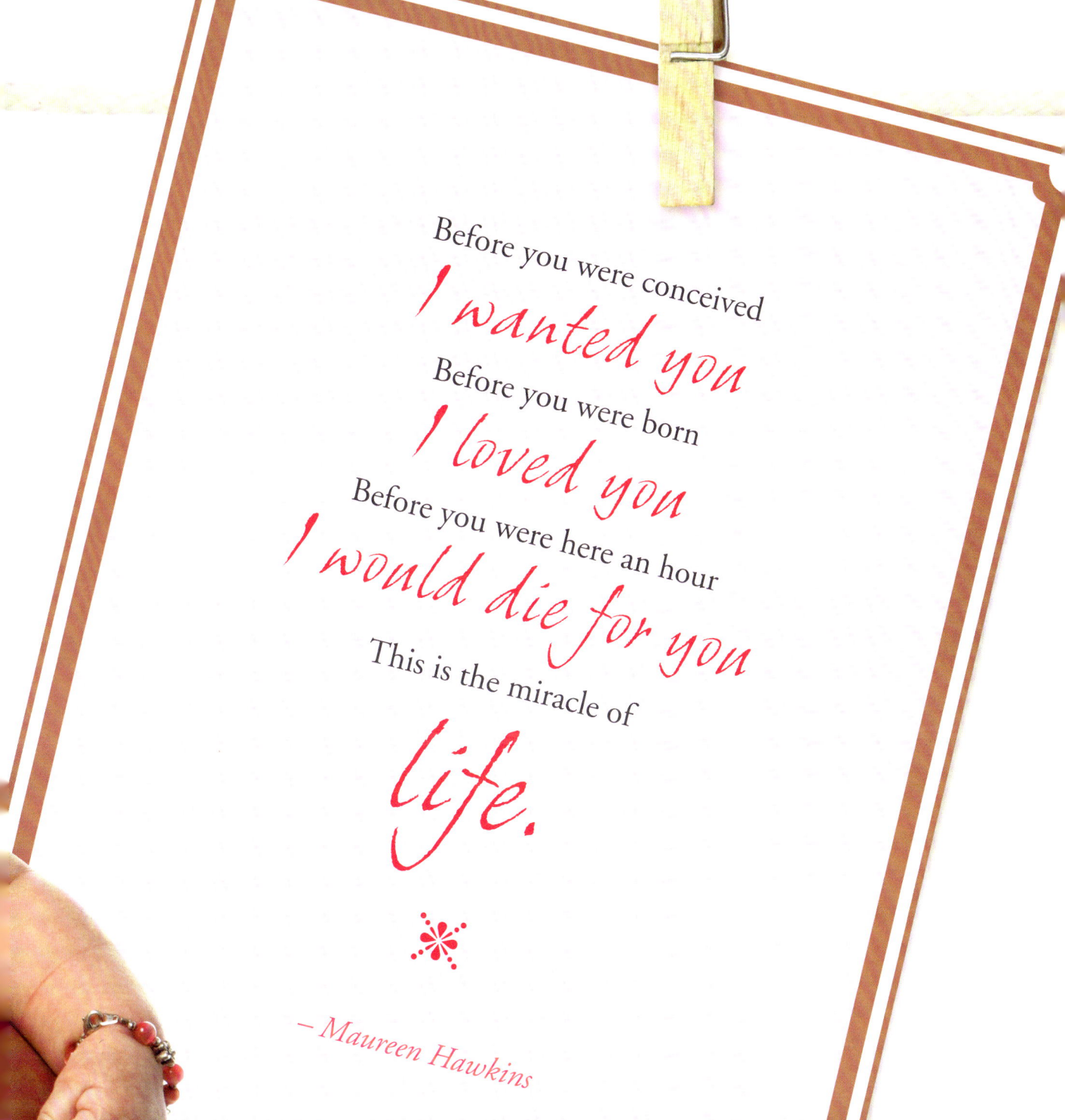

Before you were conceived

*I wanted you*

Before you were born

*I loved you*

Before you were here an hour

*I would die for you*

This is the miracle of

*life.*

— Maureen Hawkins

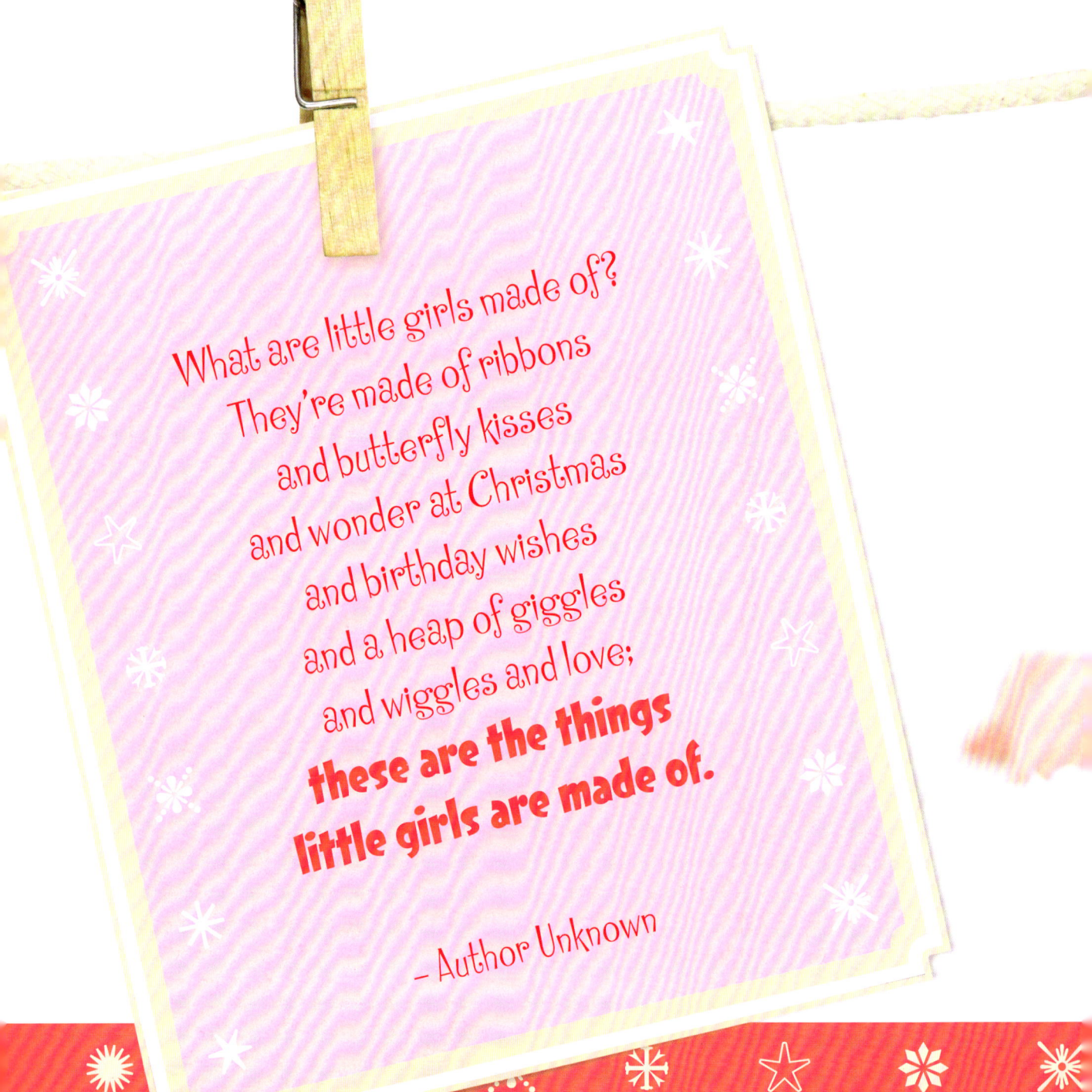

What are little girls made of?
They're made of ribbons
and butterfly kisses
and wonder at Christmas
and birthday wishes
and a heap of giggles
and wiggles and love;
**these are the things
little girls are made of.**

– Author Unknown

# Every child

comes with the message

## that God is not yet

discouraged of man.

– Rabindranath Tagore

Little girls are the *nicest* things that happen to people.

They are born with a little bit of *angelshine* about them,

and though it wears thin sometimes there is always enough left

to lasso your heart — even when they are sitting in the mud,

or crying temperamental tears, or parading up the

street in mother's *best clothes.*

*– Alan Marshall Beck*

'For I know the
plans I have for you,'
declares the LORD,
*'plans to prosper you*
and not to harm you,
plans to give you
*hope and a future.'*

*– Jeremiah 29:11*

A woman has *two smiles*

that an angel might envy —

the smile that *accepts* a lover before

words are uttered, and the smile that

*lights* on the first-born babe, and

assures it of *a mother's love.*

— Thomas C Haliburton

A baby is
**God's opinion**
that life should go on.

— Carl Sandburg

A baby will make love stronger,

days shorter, nights longer, bankroll smaller,

home happier, clothes shabbier,

the past forgotten and the future

**worth living for.**

— Author Unknown

Help me to know thy love for me,

so a loving child I may be.

With generous thoughts

and happy face and pleasant

words in every place.

Teach me to always say what's true,

be willing in each task I do.

Please help me to be good each day,

and lead me in thy

*holy way.*

# *Babies*

are God's proof that

the best things do come in

*small packages.*

— Author Unknown

We wish you soft
lullabies and smiles of joy.
Hearts that will always
listen and gentle hands to hold you
when you're afraid.
But most of all,
we wish you
love.

A *babe* in the house
is a *well-spring* of pleasure,
a *messenger* of peace and love,
a *resting place* for innocence on earth,
a *link* between angels and men.

— Martin Fraquhar Tupper

Watch over thy child, O Lord,
as her days increase; bless and guide her ...
Strengthen her when she stands;
comfort her when discouraged or sorrowful;
raise her up if she falls; and in her heart
may thy peace which passeth understanding
abide all the days of her life ...

*– Book of Common Prayer*

# Babies

are such a nice way to

## start people.

— Don Herrold

What are little girls made of?

**Sugar and spice,
And everything nice,**

That's what little girls

are made of.

**– Author Unknown**

Making the decision to have a child

*is momentous.*

It is to decide *forever* to have

your *heart* go walking around

outside your body.

– Elizabeth Stone

You made all the delicate,

inner parts of my body and knit me

together in my mother's womb …

You saw me before I was born.

Every day of my life

was recorded in Your book.

Every moment was laid out

before a single day had passed.

*– Psalm 139:13, 16*

# In love

to our wives there is **desire**,

to our sons there is **ambition**;

but to our daughters there is something

which there are **no words** to express.

— Joseph Addison

The *first* steps
a baby takes
are into your
heart.

— Author Unknown

Every child born

into the world is a

*new thought*

*of God,*

an ever-fresh and

radiant possibility.

— Kate Douglas Wiggin

*You are a marvel. You are unique.*

In all the years that have passed there

has never been another child like you.

Your legs, your arms, your clever

fingers, the way you move.

You may become a Shakespeare,

a Michelangelo, a Beethoven.

You have the capacity for anything.

*Yes, you are a marvel.*

– Pablo Casals

Life is a *flame*

that is always

burning itself out,

but it catches *fire*

again every time

*a child is born.*

– George Bernard Shaw

A little girl can be sweeter (and badder)

oftener than anyone else in the world.

She can jitter around and stomp,

and make funny noises that frazzle your nerves,

yet just when you open your mouth she stands

there demure with that special look in her eyes.

A girl is innocence playing in the mud,

beauty standing on its head,

and Motherhood dragging a doll by the foot.

**– Allan Marshall Beck**

If a child lives with criticism,
he learns to condemn.
If a child lives with hostility,
he learns to fight.
If a child lives with ridicule,
he learns to be shy.
If a child lives with shame,
he learns to feel guilty.
If a child lives with tolerance,
he learns to be patient.
If a child lives with encouragement,
he learns confidence.

If a child lives with praise,
he learns to appreciate.
If a child lives with fairness,
he learns justice.
If a child lives with security,
he learns to have faith.
If a child lives with approval,
he learns to like himself.
If a child lives with acceptance
and friendship,
He learns to find love in the world.

*– Author Unknown*

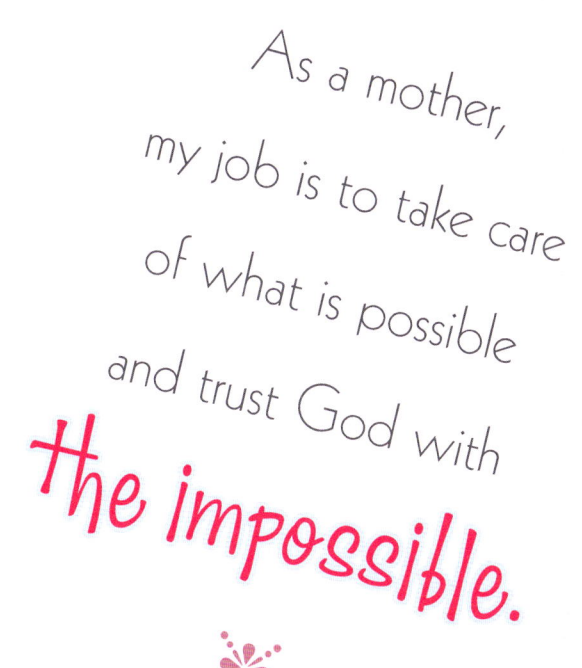

As a mother,
my job is to take care
of what is possible
and trust God with
**the impossible.**

– Ruth Bell Graham

Children are a handful

# sometimes,

A heartful

# all the time ...

– Author Unknown

Babies fill a

**hole**

in your heart

that you never

knew existed.

— Author Unknown

Before I got married

I had **six** theories

about bringing up children.

Now I have **six** children

and **no** theories.

— John Wilmot

My dear child, you are the

poem I dreamed of writing;

the masterpiece I longed to paint.

You are the shining star I reached

for in my ever hopeful quest for

life fulfilled … You are my child.

Now with all things

I am blessed.

– Author Unknown

When they placed

you in my arms,

you slipped

into my

**heart.**

– Author Unknown

A baby is teddy bears,

rattles, powder and pins,

meals at midnight ...

*giggles*

and grins.

There is an enduring tenderness that is the love of a mother.
It is neither to be chilled by selfishness, nor daunted by danger . . .
She will sacrifice every comfort to her convenience.
She will surrender every pleasure to her enjoyment.
She will glory in her fame and exalt in her prosperity.
And if adversity overtake her,
she will be the dearer to her by misfortune.
And if disgrace settle upon her name,
she will still love and cherish her.
And if all the world beside cast her off,
she will be all the world to her.

*— Washington Irving*

The father of a righteous
man has *great joy*;
he who has a wise [daughter]
*delights* in [her].

May your father
and mother be *glad*;
may she who gave
you birth *rejoice!*

— *Proverbs 23:24–25*

Babies are **always**

more trouble than you thought

**– and more wonderful.**

— Charles Osgood

When the *first baby* laughed for the *first time*, the laugh broke into a thousand pieces, and they all went skipping about, and that was the beginning of *fairies.*

— James Matthew Barrie

Many people have said to me,

'What a pity you had such a big family to raise.

Think of the novels and the short stories

and the poems you never

had time to write because of that.'

And I looked at my children and I said,

**'These are my poems.**

**These are my short stories.'**

*– Olga Masters*

# A Mother's Prayer

God, give me wisdom to see that
today is my day with my children.
That there is no unimportant moment in their lives.
May I know no other career is as precious,
no other work so rewarding,
No other task so urgent.
May I not defer it nor neglect it,
but, by thy Spirit, accept it gladly, joyously,
and by thy grace realise
that the time is short and my time is now,
*for children won't wait!*

– Helen M Young

Your children are not your children.

They are the sons and daughters of Life's longing for itself.

They come through you but not from you,

and though they are with you yet they belong not to you.

You may give them your love but not your thoughts,

for they have their own thoughts.

You may house their bodies but not their souls,

for their souls dwell in the house of tomorrow,

which you cannot visit, not even in your dreams.

You may strive to be like them,

but seek not to make them like you.

For life goes not backward nor tarries with yesterday.

You are the bows from which your children

as living arrows are sent forth.

The Archer sees the mark upon the path of the infinite,

and He bends you with his might

that his arrows may go swift and far.

Let your bending in the Archer's hand be for gladness;

for even as He loves the arrow that flies,

so He loves also the bow that is stable.

— Kahlil Gibran

# Wisdom for
## Moms-to-Be

- Sleep when your baby sleeps; it's the only way you'll be able to keep up.
- If someone offers to watch the baby, take the help! You may not get a chance to take a long, relaxing bath for a while.

- Every mother doubts herself. There is no point in comparing yourself to other mothers. Every child is different and you will find your own creative solutions. Doing your best is more than enough.
- Enjoy your baby as much as you can. Household chores can wait, but your baby won't be this little forever.
- Face this fact: your baby is going to wee on you and pretty much every-thing else when you least expect it.
- Bad dreams go with the territory. You will have dreams that something unpleasant happens to your child. This happens whether your child is 4 months or 40 years old.
- Work on being patient. It will save you a lot of stress in the long run.
- Trust yourself. Not every bit of advice you hear will apply to your child. Get to know your baby and trust yourself to make the best decisions.
- Meet your child's eyes. There is a beautiful, little soul in there who loves to be seen.
- Touching is as important as feeding. Stroke and massage your baby's skin as often as you can.
- Don't forget to take photographs!
- Get fit. As soon as your child can crawl or run you will need to be very quick on your feet.
- Keep a baby journal. Record all those precious moments. It will mean a lot to you and your child in years to come.
- There is a difference between being a good mom and being a superwoman. Superwomen end up exhausted and resentful while good moms ask for help when they need it.

'Sometimes,'
said Pooh,
'the *smallest* things
take up the **most**
room in your heart.'

– AA Milne

Every child
**begins**
the world again.

– Henry David Thoreau

# A father

is a fellow who has

replaced the currency

in his wallet with

the snapshots of

## his kids.

— Author Unknown

When babies look

beyond you and *giggle*,

maybe they're seeing

*angels.*

— Quoted in
*The Angels' Little Instruction Book*
by Eileen Elias Freeman

# A New Mother's Prayer

Lord, thank you for the ability to enjoy this
child we received from You more and more every day,
for being able to cherish and adore her.
How overwhelming your words about our children:
that with this little child we have also welcomed You into our
home; that You are here, the quiet listener who hears what
we tell this little one about You; the invisible Guest who sees
with what spiritual food we feed this child of your love.
Bread of Life, feed me, so I may feed this child with
everything that comes from You. Eternal God,
thank you that I can see myself in relationship with
You as I look at this baby: beloved, welcome child;
never deserted; cherished and safe.

Having a child is surely the most

**beautifully irrational**

act that two people in love

**can commit.**

— Bill Cosby

Babies are bits of

# stardust,

blown from the

# hand of God.

— Barretto

Babies **control** and
**bring up** their families
as much as they are
**controlled** by them;
**in fact,**
the family **brings up** baby
by being **brought up**
**by her.**

— Erik H Erikson

In the *sheltered simplicity* of the first days after a baby is born, one sees again the *magical closed circle*, the *miraculous sense* of two people existing only for each other, the *tranquil sky* reflected on the face of the mother nursing her child.

– Anne Morrow Lindbergh

What good mothers and fathers

**instinctively feel**

like doing for their babies

is **usually best** after all.

– Benjamin Spock

Loving a baby is a
**circular business,**
a kind of feedback loop.
The more you give

the more you get and the

more you feel like giving.

**– Penelope Leach**

You are

**more perfect**

than I could have hoped,

*more beautiful*

than I could have dreamed,

**more precious**

than I could have imagined …

We would like to hear from you.
Please send your comments about this book to us at:
reviews@struikinspirationalgifts.co.za

For exciting new releases and to buy online,
visit www.struikchristianmedia.co.za

STRUIK INSPIRATIONAL GIFTS

BEAUTY. PASSION. INSPIRATION.

www.struikinspirationalgifts.co.za